Involve Me
...and I will understand

CHRISTOPHER BRAMLEY

TRAINING TIPS & TECHNIQUES

FOR ENGAGING STUDENTS

First paperback edition printed 2015 in the United Kingdom
First e-book edition distributed 2014 from the United Kingdom

Copyright © 2014 Christopher Bramley.

The moral right of the author has been asserted.

All rights reserved.
No part of this book shall be stored, reproduced or transmitted in any form or by any means, electronic or mechanical, including photocopying, recording, or by any information retrieval system without written permission of the publisher or respective owners, nor be otherwise circulated in any form or binding or cover other than that in which it is published and without a similar condition being imposed on the subsequent purchaser.

Published, Designed and Set by Sanctum Publishing
For all enquiries please contact local book providers or email: info@sanctumpublishing.co.uk
Some images Copyright © 2014 Sanctum Publishing
www.sanctumpublishing.co.uk

A CIP catalogue record for this book is available from the British Library.

ISBN 978-0-9931273-2-8

Although every precaution has been taken in the preparation of this book, and every reasonable attempt has been made to achieve complete accuracy of the content in this book, the publisher and author assume no responsibility for errors or omissions, or the use of or inability to use any or all information contained in this publication; the information provided herein is provided "as is". Neither is any liability assumed for damages resulting from the use of the information contained herein. They make no representation or warranties with respect to the accuracy or completeness of the contents of this book and specifically disclaim any implied warranties of merchantability or fitness for any particular purpose, and shall in no event be liable for any loss of profit or any other commercial damage, including but not limited to special, incidental, consequential, or other damages.

The information, stories and examples contained in this book are the opinion of the individual author based on personal observations and years of experience. Your particular situation may not be exactly suited to the examples illustrated here and therefore you should adjust your use of the information and recommendations accordingly. Please use this information as you see fit, and at your own risk.

All trademarks, service marks, product names or named features are assumed to be the property of their respective owners, and are used only for reference. There is no implied endorsement in the use of one of these terms.

Please also be aware that nothing in this book is intended to replace common sense, legal, medical or other professional advice, and is meant to inform and entertain the reader.

Special thanks to Smashbox for use of Chinese Spoon image.

Contents

Introduction

Chapter 1: Basics 1
    How Confucius still applies 2
    Deep Ending? 4
    But what about Technology? Does this change how Confucius's saying applies? 4
    Why this training is different 5
    Why we should learn like children 8
    Summary 9

Chapter 2: Structure 11
    Curriculum 12
    Structure 13
    The first day and beyond 14
    Introductions 16
    Why do we need 'Elbow Room'? 16
    Pace 18
    So why is Class Size an issue? 18
    Summary 19

Chapter 3: Relations 21
    Personal connections and class atmosphere 22
    Be mindful of cultures and students 23
    Should students need rewards? 24
    Tangents and going off topic 26
    Breaking Good 27
    Summary 29

Chapter 4: Inspiration 31

Presentation! And how not to… 32
  Why is interest key to teaching? 34
  The importance of being earnest 35
  Should a teacher be a guru? 36
  Passion produces 37
  How can I increase retention of information? 38
  Summary 40
Chapter 5: Students 41
  Students drive the class 42
  How do I engage a difficult student? 43
  Patience is a virtue 45
  Showing students the door 45
  Why the cram production line approach does not work 47
  USE IT OR LOSE IT 48
  Summary 49
Chapter 6: Delivery 51
  Why should I be as concise as possible? 52
  Be like water, my friend 54
  Questions, questions, questions 55
  What about the answer? 56
  Balance in all things 57
  Summary 58
Chapter 7: Teachers 59
  Training and teaching defined 60
  Techniques for learning – what does the instructor have to practice?
  62
  The importance of repetition 64

Getting the work done 66
Keeping to the schedule... 67
Training dirty?... 68
Summary 69
Chapter 8: Supplements 71
Remote or Face to Face?.. 72
Hand-outs and why I don't use them 73
The importance of Feedback 75
How do you handle criticism? 76
Is teaching REALLY the best way to learn?........................... 77
Summary 78
Last thoughts 79

Introduction

What is this book about?

I have been on a variety of formal courses designed to teach me things in life. Some were more effective than others. School was one of the first, and there were others; how to swim, how to drive, and then eventually in IT how to do things within a highly competitive industry where knowledge and capabilities have a typical 3 year obsolescence cycle.

A great deal of courses I have attended have not been very effective. I was not good at school in many things because I was not *engaged*. It wasn't until I was taught by an English teacher named Geoff Daniel that I understood teaching could be different and make it interesting enough that I genuinely wanted to learn; not to pass some nebulous future exam I didn't understand at that age, but because I wanted to *know* things.

This is not as formal as a *Train the Trainer* or *Teach the Teacher* process; I wouldn't presume. It's just techniques I have found to work well.

What's wrong with school?

Nothing – with the pure purpose. However the implementation can leave a lot to be desired. A single excellent, interesting teacher can be a difference between a pass or a fail. A bad teacher can put you off a subject for life.

The *way* in which we are taught academically probably only suits 40% of students. The rest have to struggle with the format. Teacher constraints and political correctness often add to this, making the process a mish mash of policy which ultimately only partially succeeds in many cases.

Is this for adults or children?

Either. Although I am primarily using IT training as an example the theory is applicable with some minor differences to any class. The core principles apply when you teach anyone. Adults – especially a room of experts – bring their own challenges, whereas children have a different management approach, but in the end you are engaging, interesting, and encouraging students to learn whatever their age or experience.

How does this apply to IT training?

I believe every day, in every way, we are subject to learning. When you stop learning, you stop evolving. Being taught industry standard techniques to implement data protection with a particular solution is simply another thing to learn. IT is an interesting field to teach in, because thing change so rapidly and you are often trying to teach a room full of industry experts, which keeps you very much on your toes.

So, this is a book about IT Training?

Nope! Just the techniques, which can be applied to any training or teaching.

What defines a GOOD teacher?

There are a number of things that define a teacher from someone who merely gives you information. The two roles are often and easily confused; but a teacher makes people *want* to learn. In fact one reason I advocate smaller classes is because when you are not spread too thin you can achieve a different level again, that of mentoring.

The other thing that defines an excellent teacher is that they should learn as much as the students, every time they run a class. You never stop learning, and a teacher is included in that.

So, why are you writing this book?

Good question. The specific subject I currently teach is only applicable to one specialized area of IT, in theory (an interesting term, in computing; it means pretty much the diametric opposite of what it means in science). But in practice ANYTHING you teach can be taught in a variety of ways, and a good teacher can take any subject they understand and use techniques to effectively teach others quickly and efficiently.

This is a book about the techniques I believe work. I have been told by students that I should train people how to train, that my course was the most enjoyable they had been on and they had learned a lot more than expected, so this book largely goes towards trying to explain how I get good results.

I like helping people. I like teaching people things I have had experience of in a way that benefits them, and help them understand the *whys*. I do this in the gym, at rock climbing, in my IT training courses, wherever; and I love it when people also teach me things. We only have a finite amount of time in life, and we are learning machines; so we should learn!

Does that mean you are the perfect teacher?

Good Lord, no. I get stuff wrong all the time. I don't have all the answers. I don't have a perfect class all the time every time, and I certainly was never taught how to train and marked on it like many of my friends who teach day in day out for a living. I am going on the basis of several things: excellent feedback from the courses, compliments on the methodology, and intuition. In a nutshell, results. This is the best way I ever learned anything, and in implementing it for others it has worked for them too.

CHRISTOPHER BRAMLEY

"Tell Me and I Will Forget; Show Me and I May Remember; Involve Me and I Will Understand."

- Reputedly said by Confucius, circa 500BC

Chapter 1: Basics

INVOLVE ME

In this Chapter we will cover:

- How Confucius still applies
- Thrown in the Deep End!
- Why this training is different
- Why we should learn like children

In every class that I "formally" run, I greet the students with a disclaimer: *This training is not like other training you may have had.* It is not like, for example, a Microsoft course for MSCE certification. I explain the differences and stress that this is a fairly informal class. I explain why I think we should train the way we will over the next 2-4 days, and the reasons behind my methods.

I then apologise in advance for the PowerPoint presentation I am about to show, which is usually a promise of boredom and slumber to the average techie.

The wording may be different sometimes, but the idea is the same – I don't want people to sit down and think, *here we go. Another boring course.* It shouldn't matter what I am teaching, I want it to be interesting and as enjoyable as possible. They should be eager, not wish it is over already.

Invariably, I end up telling people the quote by Confucius, and explain why it is so important.

How Confucius still applies

In every training, I learn more and more every time and I have found the saying attributed to Confucius is still totally applicable: if I simply tell people something, they will either not listen, or forget. If I show them, demonstrate things, they might recall all or part of it (or none!). If I get them to do the work, however, and explain as they operate what is going on, the likelihood of them grasping and retaining the information is exponentially higher.

This is because humans are doing creatures. For all our abstract thinking and philosophies, nearly everyone has to DO something to prove it or learn it. Otherwise we wouldn't need around 10, 000 hours to become truly skilled at something – we could just think about it a lot.

Telling someone something has always been tenuous at best. For all the ages of man, the spoken word has changed from person to person, which is where writing became very useful for recording factual information. You also cannot force someone to listen; hearing is important to us, but not our primary sense. Something as simple as a daydream can switch our aural reception off, and words go in one ear and out of the other. This gets even worse if we don't want to listen in the first place.

Likewise, seeing something does not produce the results it once did. We have become inured to hours of television, chewing gum for the eyes, and we have learned over generations a skill directly opposite to our survival instincts: the ability to turn off or ignore our primary sense. In an age where we have any information or entertainment literally at our fingertips 24/7, coupled with information overload, we simply ignore what does not directly engage us.

Both of these are passive engagements; information arrives and we decide if it is important enough to notice, then important enough to actually process.

Doing, on the other hand, is totally different. Without active input from someone, the information simply pauses. The brain has to be engaged to do something new yourself; choices must be made to continue and direct results are immediately noticeable from those actions. This is how we learn not to touch fire, not to poke ourselves in the eye, and so forth; things you cannot always (for example) tell a child, but must let them experience for themselves because it is the only way they will learn.

Theoretically adults are beyond that and will intellectually take advice. However very often people will still only believe what they experience themselves, so the best way for anyone to learn is to be given the impetus and the opportunity. I like to call this *deep ending*.

Deep Ending?

Deep ending is uncomfortable, no doubt about it. We never learn, evolve or grow if we stay complacently inside a comfort zone. You must move outside it into a situation where you have to get things done, and this can happen in various degrees. Deep Ending is the nth degree; you are thrown in and you sink or swim.

That doesn't mean you can't have someone there to advise you on the best way to swim so you can apply it in real time, however, and that is what a good trainer does; give you the edge.

I have always learned fastest in this way. It's horrible, tiring, and nervous, but it's also exciting and when you get it you feel victorious. This is how I learned to work on cars, to build computers, to use a sewing machine to make a Victorian tailcoat, to break into a filing cabinet with a steel ruler, perform behind the back clap press-ups, and to do heavy squats on a bosu balance ball; you get in there cautiously but firmly under some pressure and simply get it done.

This is not quite applicable to a classroom, however, but it can be close. Nearly every human can learn to do *anything* if they have the motivation.

But what about Technology? Does this change how Confucius's saying applies?

I do not believe the advent of technology has changed this basic precept majorly. Granted, the ways in which we can now teach and learn are multitudinous, all the way from word of mouth to the latest online training techniques, but technology is still only a tool for learning.

We still all learn the same way – we process input with our brains and either remember it, or not. No matter what medium is used to impart that knowledge, we are still wired the same way. That is why some methods continue to work, and others do not.

As a tool, for example, I use cloud virtual Machines and give each student a lab to use. I then pull random students (or victims, as I invariably end up calling them) up on screen and we walk through the training together. I do not do the install and Next-clicking – what would be the point? I have done it a million times. A distinct advantage here is the students can independently work on these labs, and I can switch to anyone having a problem so the whole class can work on it.

It's still not perfect – speed issues running KVM sessions to servers running halfway around the globe can impact training – but it's light years ahead of giving someone a text book and telling them to read it for next Monday, because I am getting instant feedback on understanding as we go.

> *"Tell me and I will forget; show me and I may remember; involve me, and I will understand."*
>
> *It is simple and succinct.*

Why this training is different

There are several things that differentiate this training from any other I have attended myself:

The training is informal. I encourage people to relax, and I never have a room set up as a classroom with desks. I want people around a table, like a meeting of equals, where interactions and discussions can take place, where people can get *involved*.

It is made as fun as possible. Not all subjects are 100% interesting, but the delivery and presentation counts for a lot of this. If I can make backup software interesting and cool, then pretty much any subject can likewise benefit. If someone enjoys a course they pay attention, and get involved. The same happens if everyone is encouraged to connect, to "click". Everyone talks and we have a better time.

Questions are encouraged at any point. Questions tell me if people are alive, awake, paying attention, and interested. They also have the added bonus of there being at least a few I can't answer, every time, and that means I learn new things as well... and they keep me on my toes.

The curriculum is flexible. If we need to swap things around, or focus more on one area at the expense of something minor, we do. If the class is all from one company and they have specific scenarios they want to look at – we can. A course can be compressed into 3 days at a pinch, or it can run 4 days with plenty of spare time to go over problems or scenarios.

We have many breaks. It is oft-said that the human brain cannot effectively work for more than an hour at a time without losing focus and efficiency, so we have breaks for tea, or coffee, or chats.

Mental Parsley. Cleansing the mental palate. I find a good way to reset boredom and refocus is to go off topic completely. We end up talking about entirely different subjects, or watch a short clip, or generally laugh about something. People relax again, the mind resets, and focus is regained when we start up again.

I do NOT tell people how to click Next. This applies to any teaching and is tantamount to assuming someone is stupid. I tell them instead that I am there to explain *why* they are clicking next, the concepts of the solution, and how to fix it when it goes wrong. In IT especially you find in fact that the difficulty lies in getting a techie NOT to click Next.

I reiterate and query. Covering points I made before and asking them back forces students to remember what they did recently and helps embed the information. It is also good for lateral thinking.

I do not cram as much information in as quickly as possible to finish the course. This is important and relates to the breaks and mental parsley above. We move organically and at the pace the class dictates.

I encourage people to be creative where possible. This is sneaky as it makes the fast students feel good about racing ahead, and usually then someone breaks something, which leads me nicely into the troubleshooting. It also means people are more involved and (hopefully) are having a little more fun.

I reward them with something amusing or nice. At the end of an intense day, having a quick video of screaming goats, or pictures of things the class will appreciate (and so on) reinforces that they have done well, that the day is over and the mind is reset, and that it's something to look forward to.

I show them why the subject is worth their passion. The best subject in the world is worthless if it is boring, and if the teacher doesn't care. Showing a class the cool elements of something and how it can benefit them gets them passionate about it as well.

I pay attention to the class. What comes next, how it is delivered, how I explain things – this is all dependent on the class and who is in it, and it is a constantly changing variable.

I factor in plenty of elbow room. A good training has problems, errors, solutions. It shows the class the instructor knows what they are doing and it provides valuable learning opportunities. A clean training is a poor training. If we finish early, so much the better on the last day.

I say we will learn like children learn. Children learn intuitively. I believe that that learning is largely beaten out of us at school. I drop the education authority approved method of dull recital and work instead with understanding first the concepts, then using repetition and enjoyment to reinforce the ideas, with a very practical approach.

> *Remember: boring, information-crammed dumps by a disinterested instructor are not interesting.*
>
> *If you want people to listen, the subject must be made interesting, hands on, and enjoyable, and the trainer needs to connect with the students.*

Why we should learn like children

I mostly teach adults, so why would we learn like children? Isn't that the last thing an adult wants to hear?

Yes and no. It depends how and why you present this. I tell the class that traditional teaching doesn't work very well, and give examples. The upshot is that when we are children we learn via experience and repetition.

Compare how you learned to speak your first language to how you learned your second. For me, English was my best subject, but I picked it up very early on to a good degree. French – well, I can stumble my way through basics, but I remember nothing that I was taught at school. Even Dutch and Japanese – which I could speak reasonably well if nowhere near fluently at one point – have receded because I did not practice, but I picked those up an awful lot quicker than I ever did French by using the above technique.

When you are young you don't learn verbs and usage and structure from a book; you emulate your parents and intuitively learn, with the rules falling into place as you make mistakes. When something as beautiful and intuitive as language is formed into structures in a book to learn by rote, it becomes dull and dispassionate, another set of variables. This is why English language is a very different subject from English literature.

So, in the short time I have with the complex subject I teach, I try to emulate the simplicity and enjoyment as best I can of helping my students learn like children (and apply it as adults).

> *An excellent example of a training technique that works quickly and efficiently are the Pimsleur language courses. They use basic concepts and repetition to reinforce phrases you repeat and learn, and then move on – and then come back again, and ask what you did before. Then the course advances – and then you come back.*
>
> *Learning in this way is similar to how you learn language as a*

Summary

So, we have established that, as in the principle of Occam's Razor, the simplest explanation is often the correct or best. In thousands of years of progress the quickest and most thorough way to learn is still as you do when you are a child. Be interesting, passionate, and involve the students, and they will understand.

INVOLVE ME

"Information is a source of learning. But unless it is organized, processed and available to the right people in a format for decision making, it is a burden not a benefit."

- William Pollard

Chapter 2: Structure

In this Chapter we will cover:

- Defining the curriculum
- Course Structure
- Introductions and Day 1
- Pacing the class
- The importance of elbow room
- The impact of class size

Any course must be defined before it can be effectively delivered. A teacher must know the key points they will discuss, roughly how they will do so, at what pace, and what their buffers are.

I have a delightfully helpful colleague who ensures that we know up to the last minute who the attendees are, their emails (required for my course), and that they know to bring their own laptops. I am happy for people to take important calls and the odd mail, as long as we get the work done. The course is resilient enough for that.

Lastly… I fight an apparently endless battle to keep class sizes down. If you are pressured to train more people, run more courses, but unless there is no choice do not let the quality of the training give way to cramming people into the room, because in the end all the factors in this chapter are directly affected.

Curriculum

There are two ways a curriculum is defined: you define it yourself, or it is defined for you. There are advantages and disadvantages to both of these approaches, and for me the middle ground is usually the happiest medium.

Having a curriculum defined by a school, governing body or company gives you a baseline – a ground zero for what needs delivering. It may be a framework, or it may be a stringent and detailed structure. This is the hard part – setting what is the most effective course to learn. No one knows everything about everything, so picking the most pertinent points is very important – and what you find pertinent may not entirely coincide (for example) with what your company wants partners to learn.

However, defining your own curriculum gives you major advantages: flexibility, reactivity, deliverability, and focus. A corporate or body defined curriculum can be extremely sodden and boring compared to something constructed with intuitive learning in mind.

I have found that the best approach for most classes is to take a baseline curriculum from the company or governing body and then adapt it to benefit both yourself and the students to the best effect. This means it can be focused per class composition and chopped and changed as necessary. As long as you get the key elements across, it shouldn't matter if you don't rigidly stick to the structure.

Structure

This will vary from course to course. It's something that requires long term planning for school, but for an IT course it may be only 4 days – so you can plan precisely what should be covered at some point in those days.

In that example, I will start a little later on the first day and aim to finish around 4pm. We will have introductions, chats, find out what people know about the subject and how they want the course to benefit them, take multiple breaks, and address first the concepts and then the hands on basics. I explain why we are using the best practices and the effects they have, and show a couple of eye opening cool bits to the subject that they didn't know. I get them interested, relaxed, and enjoying what they thought was going to be BORING.

The next 3 days are more intense, starting a little earlier, but still enjoyable, with chats and breaks. Day 3 is always the heaviest, as by then we are doing advanced work and I have found this to be a good rhythm; people now understand the basics and we want to push through so that on the last day we can all wind down, have a good QA session to finish, and perhaps go home a little early.

> *An example of a 4 day basic/advanced split course:*
>
> *Day 1: Late start, relaxed atmosphere, introductions to basic course and each other, resolutions of anything disruptive, concepts and basics. Finish about 4pm.*
>
> *Day 2: Earlier start, straight in from Day 1. More technical, explore more complex subjects and scenarios. Try to finish 4-4.30pm.*
>
> *Day 3: Earlier start, introduction to advanced course, complex and advanced practical work with more involved factual detail later. Often latest finishing day.*
>
> *Day 4: Earlier start, straight in from Day 3, but more relaxed. If Day 3 went well there is not too much to cover, may finish around lunch for QA session and focus on anything else.*

The first day and beyond

On the first day we tend to begin at 10am unless a good reason is given otherwise. This means people finding their way get the chance to miss traffic, everyone gets their coffee and at least approaches alertness, and it feels more relaxed – an important way to start a course. I don't want people uptight and nervous on the first day.

The first day is for me to greet people and find out who they are, to introduce them around, to solve any technical problems and ensure that everyone has VM access, and to impart the core concepts of the subject. It is kept simple and interesting, with a concept PowerPoint slide

Subsequent days we start at around 9.30am, late enough that it is still relaxed and gives a bit of post-rush hour movement, but with a bit more room. We cover more complex topics and progress logically, still with breaks and relaxation but working logically through the curriculum. Each day we may finish a touch later, and it is not uncommon for a quick class to push on and cover something from the next day if they are happy to do so.

The intensity of the work increases as the course progresses, but it is ramped up organically with the class driving it, so it is rare to find a student not retaining the information as we progress. This load can be seen in the chart *Figure 1*.

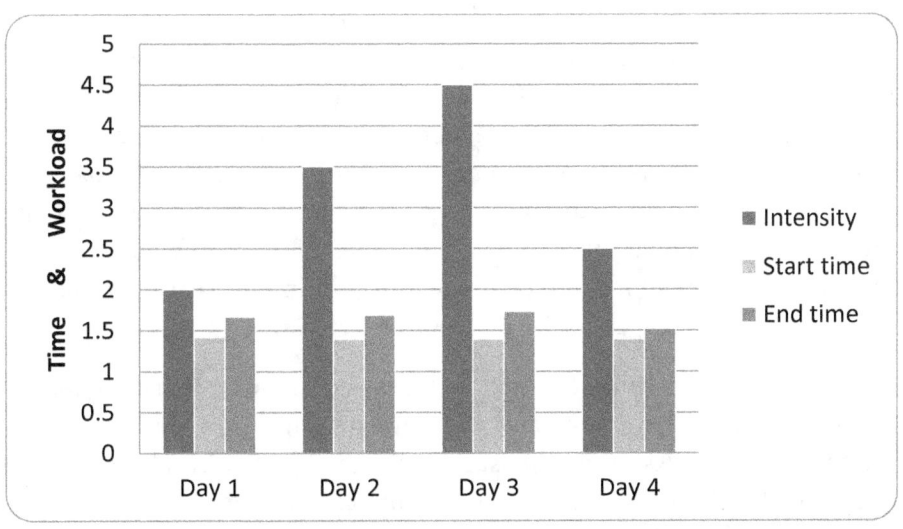

Figure 1

This is expandable to the long term, of course; the key parts here are the ramp in, gaining and maintaining interest, and the intuitive increase of workload and complexity going forward. Then rather than finishing on such complexity that attendees are left reeling and stuffed to the gills, we relax, cover any final points, have lunch, and disperse when they are happy to do so.

Introductions

This is a very important part of the first day, for a number of reasons. It helps the teacher to put faces to names, it helps everyone in the room know who each other are, and most importantly perhaps it allows people to BOND. I have seen rival partners on the course chatting and joking, helping each other troubleshoot, and swapping emails at the end. Being competitive is a good way to progress, but it doesn't mean people can't be good natured about it.

This also allows me the opportunity to introduce myself to the class. I have met trainers in the past who gave their name and cracked on, but I don't want to be a faceless instructor giving orders. I am conversant in a subject and can impart knowledge on it to the class, and therefore it is very important that they see me as a person, identify that I have and do suffer the same pain points with the subject they have, and that they trust that I am capable of training them. Getting on well with them is important to me personally as it is within my nature, but it is a secondary concern against the primary objectives.

I find that a round-robin of introductions is fine, but rather than let everyone mutter their name and a job title, it helps draw people out a little to be active. Ask them questions, chat, be CASUAL about it, and people will feel more at home rather than being under the spotlight.

Why do we need 'Elbow Room'?

Having a curriculum capable of being malleable and flexible would not be possible without elbow room built into it – spare time *just in case*. This is imperative for a course, and unfortunately management or sales may not see this is important. In their view, you should be cramming information in as fast as you can, use up every valuable minute. Of course, the human brain doesn't learn well like that most of the time.

There are other factors in any course as well. You have to cater for not only technical difficulties, an overabundance of questions, or (if you are unlucky or unwise) simply having too many people to effectively train at once, but also you must remember that your job is to have every student absorb as much information as possible. This means that the class can only run as fast as its slowest member.

That is not to say anyone is stupid; some people take very detailed notes, for example. Some people think differently and you have to rewind and explain concepts in different ways until they get them. But either way, you have to be prepared for the worst – assume you will start on the first day and finish at end of day on the last, and if it works out that you finish early then so much the better.

> *Even the most generous of spare time may not be enough in all instances. I had one class with 9 people where several forgot their laptops. I had to improvise with out of date machines.*
>
> *The wireless stopped working and I nearly had to cancel as this course was heavily practical until we found an unsecured hotspot. Someone's VM died and needed re-cloning as well. This was on the first day...*
>
> *We were so far behind (not including the number of students and questions as per usual) by the time we started that we had to stay late every day to catch up, and did not finish until nearly 4pm Friday, but we got it done – just!*
>
> *Without 'elbow room', it would have been a disaster.*

Pace

Pacing isn't something you can easily anticipate. The pace of the class is different every single time I run a course.

Pace is not just constrained by the slowest student, but also by requirements, the mix of the class (if there are less questions and a class of 6, all technical, you positively fly through) and any other issues that may crop up. It changes not only by the course but by the day. A close eye must be kept on the time and the work the students are doing to calculate if the class is behind, and it is a reactive process. This is why remote work is difficult; the trainer has to set a single pace and it cannot be gauged or enforced easily.

> *It is a delicate balance to be neither too fast nor too slow and it takes practice. If I cover everything required in a day – or a session – in whatever order, then I am happy with the pace.*
>
> *I recommend regularly getting feedback to make sure it is acceptable, as you will not always be told if students cannot keep up; however, they will readily tell you if they are bored and waiting.*

So why is Class Size an issue?

I have tried training classes that have (for various reasons) numbered between 2 and 15, and after many courses on several subjects I believe the most efficient class size for detailed training, teaching and indeed mentoring is up to 8 people.

I think training often becomes mentoring below a certain number of students; you can give them not only undivided attention but craft the course to their specific needs to further help them understand. One of our other company trainers asked what I was doing that was so different, and when I explained it he said, "Oh, I get it. You are more mentoring them than just training." I realized he was correct, and it made me think about quality over quantity.

The higher you go above 8 people, on the other hand, the more chaotic a class gets; the less control you have over the flow of training, the more questions there are, and the slower the pace will be. You cannot spend so much time with people, you cannot monitor progress as well, and like it or not the quality of the training will begin to suffer in favour of the quantity of students.

In schools there is little choice and I admire my teaching friends who have to try and deliver excellent teaching over 20 or more students. I am lucky enough that I can override sales or management to ensure my training is delivered at maximum efficiency.

> *Between 6-8 is the most efficient class size I have found. It is possible to teach up to 15-20 but the quality will go down as your attention is divided, and mentoring becomes teaching.*
>
> *Anything less than 6 and although the quality is better (1 on 1 of course being the best you can get) it is not efficient if you need to train in volume.*
>
> *Train often and in small quantities, and you will maintain the quality.*

Summary

Running a course like this is a reactive AND proactive achievement. If you scope out a framework of key points and alter it day to day as required, you can juggle the pacing, breaks, and extra time to deliver the course as smoothly as possible… and all of this depends on how many people you are trying to train at once!

"We now understand that higher-level thinking is more likely to occur in the brain of a student who is emotionally secure than in the brain of a student who is scared, upset, anxious, or stressed."

- Mawhinney and Sagan

Chapter 3: Relations

In this Chapter we will cover:

- Trainer charisma and interpersonal connections
- Different cultures and class composition
- Not offending anyone
- Tangents and enjoying the course
- Breaking Good

One of the biggest bars to learning is ego. This is true for both the teacher and the students. The truth is, everyone in the room is there to learn something, and to do this effectively everyone needs to get along. The atmosphere must be conducive to learning, and no one should feel timid or uncomfortable.

This is why I also include many breaks and we randomly go off on tangents in the class as well – if I notice a student is fading out, we switch subjects or have a break and I drop the training for a few minutes. Re-engage, awaken their minds, and then you can switch back.

Students should feel happy with the subject and what they have achieved. It means you have motivated them to pay attention and increased the overall feel good factor.

Personal connections and class atmosphere

At school, on courses, and in my courses, I have found that it is vital to establish a good connection with the students. A dull trainer is ignored, and an egotistical trainer is argued with – or ignored. To inspire people you must connect with them on a personal level as well as a professional one.

Everyone in the class is a person. A teacher is no better than the students except to have a better understanding of the subject; they are there to enlighten, inspire, and motivate. This is one reason keeping a class relatively informal works well – I chat, laugh, and connect as well as I can at the start. I'm a people person, and I let them know that we can all get on as people while we learn.

It is nearly as important that everyone is relaxed enough to get on with each other. I have had troublesome students before, and they disrupt the discussions, cause bad feeling, interrupt the training, and cause me a lot of work to smooth everything as transparently as possible. Generally you find most people get on very well once you remove the constraints of a competition and ego. We are all there to learn – trainer included! – so that's what we do. People generally are quite reserved on the first morning, but by day two have opened up considerably and are ready to really dive in.

> *Keeping a lively, equal, and friendly atmosphere helps the class drive the course. Sometimes I do not even answer questions; the class discuss it out themselves logically, and that is an excellent way to learn. It also prevents people falling asleep...*
>
> *Being personable also means that students are more likely to trust explanations from the trainer, and more timid students aren't afraid to ask questions or raise issues.*

Be mindful of cultures and students

A key part of getting on with students is (surprisingly) not offending them. It is potentially easy to do; a student or trainer may say something they find funny, but which is personally or culturally insulting to the students.

Sexism, racism or general unpleasantness are unacceptable. I tend to ignore any comments that are not appropriate, and I make sure I try and steer the class in general away from any tension that might be caused by inappropriate comments before they happen.

It may not be your fault if someone says something offensive, but as the person running the course it is still your responsibility to keep everyone as happy as you can. There is nothing wrong with discussing religion in a break, for example, but keep a sharp ear out and divert the subject if it gets a little heated.

As a teacher, you must ensure that a course will be palatable for all attendees and runs smoothly. Ribbing between students that get on well is one thing, but nastiness will destroy the atmosphere and take attention from the material. This must be avoided.

> *Whilst you cannot probe the background of students before the class, just use sense. What some people think is funny about another group or type of people – however low key – may be very insulting to others, so ensure that these situations don't happen.*
>
> *Keep focused on the material and listen out for any problems in breaks. You aren't just a teacher... you are also the class diplomat!*

Should students need rewards?

Although training in itself is a reward, we are all materialistic creatures at heart. The reason techies love Expos is at least half the lure of the free gear they can inveigle from stands.

What students may receive will depend on the course, company, and so on, but on my courses (depending on the current stock and generosity of marketing) they will receive branded pens, notepads (booklets if they are particularly honoured), smartphone screen wipes, mints, and if they are lucky a USB drive. This is excellent for brand recognition and implantation before the course even starts, but it serves to remind them afterwards as well, and it gives the ultimate satisfaction of free things we all love.

The second area is more psychological and closely linked to the training itself. If you do well, you like to be rewarded. It's a standard Pavlovian response that encourages you to do well next time, and I definitely encourage this. If I think a class has done well enough (to be fair, they have little choice as my courses are deliberately heavily practical, monitored, and student driven) I will end the day with something fun or nice.

What it is directly relates to the previous two topics; it depends on class composition and relationships. In a heavily male oriented class I may pop up one or two pictures of women in bikinis, which usually evokes a reverent silence and then eagerness to come back tomorrow and really get stuck in to the subject. Equally, if there are ladies in the class I try and find out what they like beforehand, and I'm more than happy to chuck Dave Grohl, Hugh Jackman, or Johnny Depp up on screen.

I have had students who care about neither of those and have particular interests of their own, so I try and encompass those too. I have put women, men, gadgets, racing bikes, amazing photographs, or short clips on screen… whatever makes the class feel happy at the end of the day, a little incentive to cleanse their mental palate and come back again willing to learn.

> *I find this helps cement you in the minds of the class as a person as well - which is how it should be. Just take care not to offend any students. Use sense and be appropriate to the class.*
>
> *If you are unsure – don't show it!*

Tangents and going off topic

Some courses and teachers are very stringent about off topic conversation and discussion, even if it is related to the course. I think this can be counterproductive either way; if you spend too much time off topic you lose focus, but if you do not deviate one iota you also potentially miss out on valuable insights that can be raised by questions and discussion.

Going slightly off topic can generate new questions and ways of looking at things. I have had questions which have changed how I saw the subject and raised very good points from this approach, and it often brings competitive information and technologies into the discussion. It also allows students to interpret data in a way that makes sense to them.

Uncomfortable though it is when I am on the spot in front of the class, this in turn forces me to think and learn new things about both our solution and others, and teaches me how other people might think. It's a valuable lesson.

But what about going completely off topic? That's counterproductive, right? Actually, I encourage it in moderation. Because we can't concentrate for too long, it is similar to a short break – it cuts into routine and resets the mind with a fresh topic. Of course, if you spend an hour talking about something it is a major disruption, but a few minutes – especially whilst waiting for an install to finish – refreshes everyone ready to continue.

I remember one instance where a student was falling asleep as I spoke. It was the most intensive day and he had been out the night before, and concentration was drifting. I stopped talking and put up a picture of a girl in a bikini… and waited. As his focus drifted back through alertness, his eyes snapped open and he came back as if awakening from the dead. It was an impressive sight, and caused us some amusement. Then we carried on with the course.

> *Tangential or totally off topic discussion can be valuable when not uncontrolled, and can provide some much needed fun and refocusing during duller moments or waiting periods.*
>
> *They can also provide valuable insights into how other people will see the subject or how they think, and can help you understand better how to deliver information to different people.*
>
> *Just be careful not to let a discussion impair the actual training!*

Breaking Good

It is a widely agreed fact that most healthy adults and older children cannot sustain focus on a subject for more than roughly 40 minutes at a time. Humans can, however, refocus after a brief period and continue. This is why we can watch a film three hours long, or drive a car for hours on end, and why we can soldier through 7 hours of IT training on subjects that can be both fascinating and boring.

Where a lot of training goes wrong is to just keep going without any break at all. This is especially difficult in school, where you often have only an hour for a lesson and you have to try to capture easily distracted children with a proportionately shorter attention span. Realistically I see people losing focus after 20-30 minutes of an assigned task, so I try and either break or hit a tangent sufficiently removed from the task to reset the focus. A brief chat is sometimes enough, but if warranted a 10 minute coffee break is an even better option.

There are other factors that will affect this time, including how familiar someone is with the general task, tiredness, hunger, or distractions (two students loudly talking about something else, for example).

There is plenty of interesting information on attention spans and brain mapping out there, but you don't need a degree in psychology to be an effective trainer. I use myself as a litmus: if I couldn't do it, then I won't assume other people in the class can either.

Breaks are a perfect opportunity to completely clean the mental slate. At these times I tend to get into involved discussions about other subjects, or show a quick video, or ask questions about other things – anything that allows the focus to change. Since I am particularly fond of Star Wars, it is not uncommon for me to show a clip from fan edits, or if I know Minecraft players are present I may show them a scale building of Castle Grayskull I completed. It doesn't really matter what it is: as long as it interests, distracts or amuses them, cleanses the mental palate, and allows them to focus once again on the task at hand afterwards, it serves its purpose.

Lunch is also important. Quite apart from needing to eat after intense concentration, it gives people a chance to laugh, chat, discuss things from the training, meet the sales teams and others in the company, and talk business. I believe it is very important that if your course involves lunch it is good quality. People will not concentrate or be very well fuelled if the food is poor, and no trainer wants complaints about something he is not responsible for.

It also does not reflect well on the company or institution – if they can't be bothered to provide a decent feed, then how much do they care about the course and students? Not the best message.

> *Quality of breaks is as important as quality of training. They are vital to students retaining information and being happy and alert.*
>
> *Lunch is part of this. I recall one course where a student told me that a highly respected vendor in IT had run a course costing £3000 per seat for a week, and every day had served cold pasta. When they complained, the company responded "You are not here for the lunch."*
>
> *This is a terrible attitude. The lunch is part of the course, and an unhappy student will not learn effectively. It is also arrogant and uncaring.*

Summary

Clearly, it is very important to establish a good relationship from the get go with the students, and encourage the same between them as well. A good atmosphere is conducive to good training. Be mindful of the class composition and keeping everything smooth and diplomatic – it is up to you to ensure the students enjoy the class. Finally, ensure everyone gets enough rest! Break, eat, distract, chat, laugh… whatever it takes to keep focus. It sounds counterintuitive, but it really isn't, and in the long run it keeps focus smooth and the class alert and content.

INVOLVE ME

"The mediocre teacher tells. The good teacher explains. The superior teacher demonstrates. The great teacher inspires."

- William Arthur Ward

Chapter 4: Inspiration

In this Chapter we will cover:
- Presentation – and how not to
- Why interest is key
- The importance of being earnest
- Passion in teaching
- Increasing retention of points with cues

With the best will in the world, a teacher with the wisdom of ages is not a good teacher if they cannot impart that information effectively. The single most important skill I have learned and continue to try and refine with every course is the ability to break down a complex concept into simple, concise, and understandable explanations.

This is part and parcel of presentation as a whole. The presentation is how a trainer interacts with a class; it is the conduit of knowledge between teacher and student. If the teacher isn't succinct, knowledgeable, and caring about their subject, the class will find it much harder to comprehend and invest in.

The best teachers get the students excited about a subject, and that brings in an underlying skill that is not related to the knowledge of the subject – the ability to MOTIVATE.

Presentation! And how not to…

The best presenters I have seen on any subjects are those that deliver excitement, interest, and interaction with the audience. I experienced this in school, at expos, and in some trainings, but it is something that seems to be lacking in the world of IT for some reason.

The worst presentations I have experienced on the other hand have literally sent me to sleep. Reiterating points over and over again in succession, trying to drill facts on a screen into my head, and doing so without apparent interest on the trainer's part is why many people fail at successfully getting an audience to retain data.

A lot of people associate the presentation quality with the tools, and that is inaccurate. PowerPoint has a bad reputation for content delivery, for example, and this is mainly due to how it is used. In and of itself, it is a colourful and potentially interesting way to quickly deliver information, but when it is a textual list of points read out by a droning presenter, I honestly cannot think of a more boring or insulting way of being taught. This applies to any demonstration tool not used correctly, be it audio visual technology or a monotone blackboard and chalk.

What is lost with this approach is the opportunity to generate INTEREST in the subject. Use the tool intelligently; display points and talk ABOUT them, don't read out a list. I am perfectly capable of reading for myself and it annoys and disinterests me when a trainer assumes they have to do it for me. Don't have boring slides or drawings; use humour, or wow them with cool facts. Use visual cues. Encourage interaction DURING the presentation; questions are less relevant or forgotten when stacked until the end. Ask the audience if they understand what they have seen; ask them leading questions into the next subjects. Get them interested in what you are talking about!

> *Before you can give information, you must gain the student's interest, and this is ALL in the presentation.*
>
> *Don't assume your audience is stupid and bore them with text! Be dynamic, amusing, fun, and bold; use presentation tools to drive points home, but don't drone out a list. Encourage interactions, make them PART of the presentation. If you persuade students to invest, their interest will be sparked.*
>
> *I run a PowerPoint for the concepts of my courses before we get stuck in hands on, and I continually ask – does this make sense? Any questions? Are you happy with that? I jokingly apologise for the approaching "Death by PowerPoint", but the one thing I do not do is actually kill interest. If a slide is boring or irrelevant – I skip it.*

Why is interest key to teaching?

There are two levels of interest in any lesson that are required if you want students to listen. One of these is interest in you, and the other (more important) is interest in the subject.

There are those that can take in information and note it down and learn it by rote, and even understand it by analysing it, but not everyone can do that. It is very hard to effectively take information in if it is not interesting.

The teacher therefore has a twofold purpose: to be personable and interesting so that students will pay credence to what they are saying, and to adjust the student's perception (if required) to see the subject as interesting.

Some subjects are inherently interesting, and some are less so. This is true also of parts of a course; I find people are very interested in running Bare Metal Restore, for example, as it is involving and very cool (and there is a direct application to their roles, usually, to make their lives easier). In contrast heads nod a little when I go through each command executable to define Vault structure and how it runs, because it's a list of applications that do things we have largely already done – but they need to know it.

Creativity is therefore an important part of this. Allow your students to be a little creative! Don't say they all have to do the exact same thing. Let them use their own names, set up their own scenarios to demonstrate the point. Involve them, get them enjoying what they are doing, get them to invest their creativity and it all becomes inherently more interesting.

Virtually any subject can be made interesting, within reason; you also have to take into account the student familiarity with it. If someone knows backup extremely well, you can cut through the more simplistic and interest generating presentation, because they are already interested. This is something you have to judge roughly at the start of the course.

You can't please everyone – but if you do your best to make both yourself and the subject as interesting as possible, you usually find a good middle ground where people will listen and focus.

The importance of being earnest

Being earnest is crucial. For a student to take what you say on faith they must trust that you know what you are talking about and that you are telling them the truth. There is a reason techies often make sales people cringe, and that is because it is easy to err on the side of actual technical capability rather than the upsell.

Of course diplomacy is not just for student interactions; the trainer must ensure that the students are seeing the positives of the subject, so training is also a form of selling (if you do it right). But it can be truthful selling.

Be honest with your information, and if you don't know something say so. Offer to get a specific answer if you can. As important is to then demonstrate what you have taught with object lessons to prove you are teaching them correctly. People are very often slightly dubious on the first day, because the subject is new, and there are questions that seem to poke holes in it. If you prove you are earnest, knowledgeable and honest, the class will relax and take in the information quicker and with less argument.

Don't discount questions though: they are very important and show people are paying attention.

Should a teacher be a guru?

This is an interesting question. Hypothetically a teacher does not have to be a guru as a core goal is to motivate the class to effectively help teach themselves, but I believe this depends on the subject, class, and course. In IT you are in front of a room full of experts – some of whom have been working in IT to a deeper level than you for your entire lifetime – and you have to encourage them that you know what you are talking about.

There is no problem if a teacher cannot directly answer a very difficult or off the cuff question – just be honest. But you can look for answers, or in many cases talk through with the class and explain your reasoning – if you know the subject you will very often be correct and you will look very good to the students (who can smell a "quote the book without understanding" teacher a mile off). If you know only the bare minimum the class will not trust you or your ability to teach the subject.

You don't necessarily have to be the world expert on a subject, but you should know a lot about it, to a good applicable level, with practical experience. That is a fantastic base; simply teaching classes will then broaden your knowledge and deepen it.

I think anyone who delves into a subject to teach and teaches it consistently at a very interactive level will become a guru whether they intend to or not.

> *There is no shame in not knowing an answer, as long as it isn't to EVERY question. No one person knows everything about a subject. Students are usually more than happy for you to be honest and get back to them with the information later on.*
>
> *This, incidentally, is also how you learn new things on every course.*

Passion produces

Passion is the last part of this quartet. Presentation, honesty, and knowledge will get you a long way, but if you clearly do not care about the subject, why will the students? You will be giving an unconscious signal that the subject is not worth your time – or theirs.

You don't have to believe the subject is the most incredible thing since sliced bread, but you do have to show that there are parts that you think are genuinely exciting, or cool, or helpful. Drawing comparisons to your own escapades with the genre, or adding a bit of showmanship, showing you believe in it, and above all saying "Yes – this subject isn't perfect, but by god it has some awesome pieces to it!" is very encouraging to your students.

This is especially true of jaded attendees who have prior experience with other solutions that compete with yours, or who have battled issues in the field that you can at least partially solve. By showing them you believe the product can at least partially resolve this, showing you believe IN the product, and making a convincing argument as to why it is effective, you can gain the trust and interest of the class.

It is not uncommon for students to leave the class of what they thought was a week of boring technical training vitalized and eager to put this into practice, and that is what every teacher wants. You cannot get passion without passion!

> *A good example of this was an attendee who was heavily conversant in a rival solution. He asked more questions than most attendees I have taught, and argued capabilities even with clear evidence. Sometimes he was right, sometimes he was not, but despite this (and the affect it had on the training time) he left happy and admitting the solution we had was very good in many ways. He complimented my passion in defending it – when I clearly admitted parts did not do what he expected – and said he was looking forward to working with it.*
>
> *Not every argument is bad. Argue comes from "arguer", which is from the Latin "to discuss". A good argument can involve the whole class and imprint your proven answers in their minds, but you have to be passionate, interesting, and know what you are talking about – and present it well.*

How can I increase retention of information?

So, you are impassioned, motivating, knowledgeable, and you can get the idea across. Is that it?

There IS more you can do. Humans learn by association, and whilst we are perfectly capable of remembering abstract concepts it is much easier to assign a trigger to them. This is why learning anything is best done with interesting examples and easily remembered cues.

Traditionally teachers use a range of techniques for this, from acronyms to rhymes to pictures, and so forth. I find the best ones are those that really capture the attention of the student, and once again – make them invest! This is very easy to do with both audio and visual. Humour is another excellent aid, as is a good discussion – anything where you are involved, even to argue the point. You may not agree, but you will remember.

I don't just use clips for breaks and resetting the brain - I use them to drive points home as well. It doesn't actually matter what you use – a picture, a word, a situation, a joke, a video, a demonstration that grabs attention, anything that works to help people remember.

Another thing I find particularly helpful in IT are *real world* examples. An example is useless if it is not applicable.

> *An excellent example of this is with a maintenance task in some of our software. A certain situation can cause it to disable itself, which seems (on the surface) very counterintuitive, as this will cause the solution to eventually break. But there are excellent reasons for it, which I explain. I then caution against laziness and human nature, and tell students not to just try and turn it back on as it will disable itself again.*
>
> *This is all just so many words; until you are in a crisis and experience it, it won't register. So I then play a video of a Useless Box from YouTube. They exist solely to turn themselves off immediately they are turned on. I use this clip as it a) demonstrates the uselessness of arguing with a machine designed to do something, and b) it gets shouts of laughter from those who have never seen one. Lesson learned, and sunk firmly into memories.*

Summary

There are four things you must have for a student to be prepared to learn from you: passion, knowledge, their interest, and their trust. These can then be reinforced by positive cues to aid memory of specific concepts, and examples of where they can genuinely use them.

Using these you can inspire a student in any subject and help them retain key points, whether it is a history class at school or a course to determine the best data protection methods. Just remember that some subjects are inherently more interesting than others (history has more battles).

"A Teacher can only open a door; the student must enter by themselves."

- Chinese Proverb

Chapter 5: Students

In this Chapter we will cover:

- Students driving the course
- Engaging difficult students
- Patience
- Opening the door for students
- Why some courses fail
- The importance of practice

So, you have managed to reach your students, engage their interest, and start getting your ideas across. The next step is dealing with the students during this process. Students are an ever-changing landscape of individuals, and from class to class you can have wildly varying personalities.

It is important to remember that without the students there is no class, and without their participation there is no drive – at least, if you run the classes with student involvement.

Gaining their interest and trust is only the beginning; you have to keep that momentum going.

Students drive the class

If you run a practical course that relies on student involvement and interest you will quickly find that you are in fact not the one who drives the class. Without student participation the course grinds to a halt, and momentum is hard to regain.

You need to keep an eye on the class to see where someone may be falling behind, or rushing ahead, and try and balance the flow, but you should never try and wrest control of the class. You have enabled the students to perform the tasks, and given them best practices on how to do it; don't disenfranchise them by then challenging their capabilities.

A teacher is a guide for a student; you are the voice advising them how to swim most effectively as they flail in the deep end. Sometimes, you are even in there with them.

How do I engage a difficult student?

This is a very difficult question to answer and will depend entirely on the student. The word "difficult" doesn't necessarily mean they are a problem – it can be something as simple as a language or cultural barrier, or something as complex as being unfocused because of personal problems. Some people grasp certain concepts easily, and some do not.

I believe it is important to be accommodating and understanding whilst also trying to get them invested as best you can. This is not always possible; you cannot win them all, but you have to try.

There are unfortunately other precedents, however.

Are they being deliberately obtuse? Is it a personal dislike of you or the subject? Do they simply refuse to open their minds to the subject and argue everything, no matter how well proven or minor? Perhaps they didn't want to come on the course in the first place, or they arrive extremely late every day, or maybe they inform you with no notice that they won't be attending a day for some reason.

I have had all of these happen at some point in some way. This is where patience and diplomacy can be tested – I am very easy going and the class is informal, but it is unfair on the teacher and the rest of the students if these impact the course. At school this is more understandable; it is the nature of children to try and skip classes, especially when the course is over a term. But for adults representing companies that rely on revenue directly linked to this course, especially when they may have paid for them to attend, it can be insulting or unacceptable.

INVOLVE ME

With the obtuse students, or those intent of arguing everything, I use evidence and logic and refuse to argue past that. With a dislike (thankfully nothing personally of me yet) you have to just agree to disagree if they won't accept your reasons for fairly judging the subject. You can ignore any dislike of you personally; you are there to do a job and they won't see you again, so no harm done.

For students who literally don't care, I try to motivate them by pointing out that to gain partner status they need this course, and also try to adjust their perspective to see WHY this subject is so interesting. It's not unknown for a previously disinterested student to find something they think is cool and then gain their investment from that point on. Late students you have to give a few minutes and then start without after the first time, and if they will suddenly miss days (depending on their interest, capability, reason and where we are) I simply inform them that they will have to re-sit that part of the course to be accredited.

If you cannot find a peaceful way to resolve any of the issues, the next best step is to diplomatically ignore them, or confront them logically and politely but firmly. You can't MAKE a student respect you, and sometimes people just will not care enough whatever you do.

> *If people REALLY want to, they will find fault with anything. Don't argue with disruptors – it is counterproductive. Try everything you can to involve them, and you may be surprised – sometimes someone is just having a bad day! Otherwise, you have to be polite, firm, and diplomatic, and ensure you do not neglect the rest of the class. The good of the many outweighs the good of the few, or the one – as a certain pointy-eared science officer once said.*

Patience is a virtue

It is thankfully far more common to find students who genuinely want to learn but are having trouble for whatever reason; deliberately difficult students are quite rare.

The key skill on an ongoing basis – especially when trying to impart concepts to a class – is patience. Some people grasp things very quickly. Some forget as quickly. Some take a long time and multiple ways of explaining it to get it, but once in their heads it stays. Some people, whether through experience or nature, grasp concepts very fast and remember them. Some seem to simply not grasp certain things at all and forget it even when they finally do.

Because you will always have a mix of these students in the class you must learn two skills; patience and the ability to simplify a concept in multiple ways. If a student cannot grasp it one way, rewind and explain it another way. Draw examples, give case studies, and get the class involved in helping explain it. Your patience is always rewarded when a face lights up in understanding.

Showing students the door

It was not until I began teaching that I truly understood the saying that you can open a door for students but they must walk through themselves. I had never realised that my love of learning things had often been blocked by this misunderstanding.

When you don't realise it's a door opened for you to walk through, you sometimes ignore it, or don't clearly realise the ramifications of not walking through. I very much wish that this had been explained clearly and simply to me at school – in my mid-teens I did not understand these things and the process was very opaque. I was a child being forced to adult decisions that could affect the rest of my life without any true comprehension.

To take the analogy further, I was pressured into choosing economics, which is something I am not suited for at all, and I tried to change to music and was denied by the school (for numbers and curriculum reasons I seem to recall). That was a door shut in my face, and I have always regretted it.

This is why I believe choice and the understanding of that choice is very important – I make it clear that not gaining accreditation will directly affect their company status, and also their ability to do their job, so it is beneficial to them. If you don't care, or you cheat, you are only cheating yourself – you won't be able to apply the knowledge in the real world, and THAT is the entire point!

Further, I believe that students in the classes I run should help or teach others what I teach them. Students helping explain is simply the best way for them to understand and bed in the concepts within the class, and this is why this kind of class discussion is particularly valuable. It is fantastic to watch a class arrive at the correct conclusion with little or no input from me through discussion and interest, and they will remember it.

Once a student understands that the door is there, there is incentive to step through.

Teaching an old dog new tricks IS possible. Students CAN push past their limits and move outside their comfort zones to great benefit. ANYONE can learn, given the impetus and inspiration – no matter their age or capability.

All they have to do is step through the door – and keep walking.

Why the cram production line approach does not work

When you are forcing information into students without slowing, and pushing the pace regardless of how they learn – in essence, driving them – you will miss the nuances of their feedback and they will miss the nuances of the training.

Many classes in school are like this. Every IT course I have been on has been like this. You get into the room and then the instructor talks to you, presents, demos processes, makes you run a few exercises, and usually almost verbatim recites the huge bundle of printed steps that may or may not be useful reference. The courses are detail heavy, long and intense, have few breaks, and sometimes the trainer is clearly not even invested in running the class.

It is a business process; get students in the door, get through the course, get them out on time, done. Next class. This is not a good approach. Students are individuals, and not all equal in experience or manner of learning; if you do not organically work with the class as people, you will not get the best out of the course and neither will they.

Some courses and teachers are definitely better than others, but there is a reason cram sites get so much attention. Courses are often devalued because they become less about practical experience and application, and more about short-term cramming to pass an exam and end up with a certificate.

Don't get me wrong; to pass a school exam, you must have paid *some* attention. To become Cisco certified, you must be able to remotely configure routers with IPv4/6 subnets of the correct class. But often you aren't given flexibility in how you approach the task in the course, or get left behind and struggle with notes afterwards. On the flip side, I have met many worthy Microsoft certified people in my time... and I have also met my fair share that have the qualification and don't know what they are doing with it!

If you can, build flexibility and buffers into the class so you can ensure EVERYONE leaves understanding what they have done.

Lastly, this approach – combined with the DEMAND that students learn – produces pressure, which is not optimum for learning. Stress does not induce good retention of data or a smooth class. The main reason I make a class fairly informal is it removes the stress and the "cram" mentality, and relaxed students take in a lot more.

> *"I think the big mistake in schools is trying to teach children anything, and by using fear as the basic motivation. Fear of getting failing grades, fear of not staying with your class, etc. Interest can produce learning on a scale compared to fear as a nuclear explosion to a firecracker." – Stanley Kubrick*

USE IT OR LOSE IT

The last part to the learning is continuing the skills. Like language, like flexibility, like a car left sitting in a garage, like a singing voice, like a time limited voucher - use it or lose it!

This applies to any skill you learn. You can, with enough practice, retain either pattern memory or (physically) muscle memory, but it is NOT the same as regular practice.

When students leave the class I urge them to do two things before they sit the exam. First, I suggest they leave the course a week, and allow what we have done to sink in. This is a verified tactic for memory retention; it has been proved that students do better in exams if they read up 24 hours before sitting an exam and sleep on it than if they cram up until the last minute.

Second, I strongly recommend that they practice what they have learned on the course. 4 days is NOT enough to teach people to be experts, however quick they are; even a term for children is not enough (in fact, given the diversity of subjects, it may be too much as the focus spreads over time).

> *The ONLY way to become truly proficient at anything and reach your fullest potential is to practice! Play around, BREAK whatever you are doing, remember how you fixed it and learn more yourself. Use it, and you will not only keep it, you will improve it. Successful people know how to fail; it is how they learn success.*
>
> *"...to learn and not to do is really not to learn. To know and not to do is really not to know." – Stephen R. Covey*

Summary

I believe it is very important for the students to drive the class, not the teacher; you are a guide, not a disciplinarian (unless they are unruly children, in which case you are both!). In line with this, you must exercise patience, inspiration and interest to engage all the students, and work hard to engage difficult students. It is very easy to ignore them; you aren't paid to have an easy time, however.

Unless it is at the expense of the class, you owe it to everyone to engage them all. Encourage them to learn and practice their new knowledge, and treat each course as a fresh experience and the students as new people, and you may be surprised at how many students walk through the door you hold open for them.

INVOLVE ME

"True teachers are those who use themselves as bridges over which they invite their students to cross; then, having facilitated their crossing, joyfully collapse, encouraging them to create their own."

- Nikos Kazantzakis

Chapter 6: Delivery

This chapter, we will cover:

- Why being concise is best
- Reactivity in class
- Questions
- Achieving balance

As important as the ways of reaching the students themselves are the ways you form the delivery for yourself. The teacher must understand how to dynamically work with the class, encouraging questions and delivering the information as succinctly as possible.

This is not just for the benefit of the class – the trainer can gain at least as much from a course as the students, in either material knowledge or understanding of applying their skills to make the next class even better. But this also helps you prepare the students to be teachers themselves – involve them fully and their questions – and answers – will start to be considered so that others understand.

Why should I be as concise as possible?

It is very easy to explain things in a complex manner. You get all the information in the words, you can cover all eventualities... and you can lose or bore students, or they simply won't remember the explanation.

One of the skills every teacher learns sooner or later is to answer as simply as possible. When you use clarity and simplicity in descriptions, people remember the concepts much better and more clearly, and understand them more quickly. You also increase the pace of the class.

Twitter is an excellent tool for clear, precise and compact concepts you wish to get across – you have 140 characters, so you had better make it count. Think about each concept you teach in the same way. You can't spend forever explaining things, and you will stop the flow of learning if you make it too incomprehensible. Also, clarifying and simplifying the information forces you to think closely about it, and the process itself enhances your understanding dramatically.

For example, I knew how retentions and seed migration worked in our software – but it wasn't until I had to explain this to multiple classes, with each asking different questions and understanding it at different levels, that I realised exactly how at a deeper level it works and how applicable it is.

This is an optimisation process that benefits you AND the class. You deliver concepts clearly, quickly, and memorably, and they remember them and take them in more easily. Think back to the last snappy advertising slogan you heard, and then imagine it was a rambling discourse expounding the product's virtues. I know which sends me to sleep more quickly and which I remember.

> *A good example of this is how I explain the difference between two forms of data protection. I ask the class, "What would you say the difference is between backing up and archiving?" The responses I get range from a shrug to a vastly complicated explanation about migrations and data copies. I then address the answers, and say, "Even simpler than that." It is rare anyone gets the right simple answer here.*
>
> *I then say, "The only real difference between a Backup and an Archive is that one is a COPY, and the other is a MOVE." This is short, simple, and very easy to remember, and it is a light bulb moment for a techie (it was for me). You KNOW the answer, but you didn't realise you knew it.*
>
> *"That is what learning is. You suddenly understand something you've understood all your life, but in a new way." – Doris Lessing*

Be like water, my friend

A situation that really forces this optimal delivery of concepts is being on the spot and having to react in real time. This is the teacher's own peculiar form of deep ending, and requires flexibility and reactivity.

Students, bless them, ask decidedly awkward questions. I do when I am a student. My students do it to me. It is how we understand things, and your mind may not work like theirs. You may not always have the right answers, complete answers, or sometimes ANY answers.

You have to be VERY fast on your feet in a room full of professionals. Lateral thinking, reactivity and flexibility in the curriculum to allow for these things is actually better in many cases than vast knowledge; I have learned new things about the subject on the fly because I was asked a question in real time, I didn't know, and I proved the process to myself and the class intelligently. I NEVER forget those lessons, and neither do the students.

If your course is run by script and at your pace not theirs, you had better hope your knowledge is positively encyclopaedic if a query arises because you won't have the opportunity to work it out. The best you can do here is say you don't know and come back to them with the answer – hardly a problem, but I prefer to at least try and answer, for my benefit and theirs. I'm not always able to but I constantly surprise myself.

Of course, it is not always enough to be fast on your feet either – know your subject and the questions you may get and you get a jump start on the queries. Then you can investigate as needed, and be prepared to apply that lateral thinking and prove to the class you are capable and know what you are teaching. Nothing will cement their faith in you like admitting you don't know and then solving the problem in front of them anyway with an explanation afterwards of what happened. At that point, you are all learning together.

> *Be like water. Flow around problems, using the elbow room you build into a class. Assume the shape of each individual class and don't try to force the class to you, and you will find you can react quickly and flexibly to most situations.*
>
> *"You must be shapeless, formless, like water. When you pour water in a cup, it becomes the cup. When you pour water in a bottle, it becomes the bottle. When you pour water in a teapot, it becomes the teapot. Water can drip and it can crash. Become like water my friend." – Bruce Lee*

Questions, questions, questions

Questions are a sign you are doing things right. Too many questions can interfere with the class, and may not be genuine (I have had questions from the same student over and over again designed to show that they know things purely for their own "status" in the training, and that benefits no one except their own fragile ego), but real questions are a very positive part of the course.

Questions show that students are paying attention, that they are interested, that they are trying to understand. If they didn't care about the subject, they wouldn't ask. Questions can also show that they are trying to solve problems practically – very often, I will get a scenario and then a "how would I do this?" This allows us to go outside the basics of the class and use real world situations as examples.

They allow students with similar mind-sets to gain an understanding more easily as well. If three people in the class are not quite following an explanation, and one asks a valid question, the specific focus of the question forces me to address part of the explanation they may be having trouble with, and often then the others also "get it".

Questions also allow other students the opportunity to enter a discussion where (potentially) the entire class can get involved. This is where sitting in a meeting style around a table rather than in a classroom setting is vital, as it encourages interaction on an equal level, and when the class themselves answer questions and solve troubleshooting, they remember it and gain a real sense of achievement.

The final thing that questions do is give the trainer an opportunity to learn as well. I believe questions should be asked as and when they occur, and not saved until the end. They will then stay relevant in everyone's minds, and if students wait they might forget to ask something important.

Finding the answers to questions – especially in class through application of current knowledge – is like automatically levelling up towards guru status.

> *One of many good examples was where I had been told something about the solution I was teaching, years ago, and a question was asked that challenged what I knew. I had been teaching something I understood but had not investigated enough to the depth I required to answer the question. Eventually most of the class was involved in the discussion, and we all found together that the truth was slightly different than my understanding of what it did. My understanding grew with theirs.*

What about the answer?

That is the most important point of the questions for me. It doesn't matter what the answer is or where it comes from – I learn from the questions and it benefits me at least as much as the class.

Do not let fear or ego stand in your way of learning. It is easy to outline or bypass something you are unsure of; deep-ending during a class is a fantastic way to understand a subject you are unsure of beyond a certain point. I have learned more from difficult questions than I have from just prepping a course, and being kept on my toes keep me from being complacent and falling into rote. It also keeps you humble and reminds you that *you do not know everything.*

Think about that for a minute. No one person can know everything, so you should be open to new data, to evolving your depth and breadth of understanding in a subject.

It could be a question from a student, or something a colleague says which clicks. You may be explaining something and suddenly realise a deeper meaning, a new way to explain. Whatever it is, you should be even more open to the window of learning than the class. You will grasp the concept quicker and understand its place better, and you must never assume you know it all.

> *Be honest, be humble, and be happy to learn at every chance you get.*
>
> *"Whoever ceases to be a student has never been a student." – George Iles*

Balance in all things

The danger of questions of course is that they can disrupt the flow of the class, and they can also be used to stroke egos rather than truly gain knowledge.

As always, as the teacher your job is to also try to maintain a delicate balance in the class. Encourage questions, answer questions, but don't let a student hog your time with them. Diplomatically move to other student's questions as well. Get an even spread if possible.

Don't let discussions or multiple student questions get out of hand, either. If a student asks a lot of questions you will come to later, say so! I usually answer a quick one that will be addressed if it is relevant, but otherwise I say "we are going to get to that later." Students appreciate it if you get to it and then reference back to their question; ask them if this has answered it, when you get there. It shows you are paying attention to them, too.

Summary

Be focused and economical with your explanations, and keep them short, catchy and simple. Imagine how a prophet would sound if their parables were complex and hard to understand or remember – they would gain few followers!

Stay flexible and reactive, and absorb disruptions rather than allow them to damage the class. Questions should provide impetus to drive class understanding, but make sure they don't get in the way of the course itself. And don't forget – keep your mind open to learning as well. You will be amazed how much you take in whilst teaching others.

"Spoon feeding in the long run teaches us nothing but the shape of the spoon."

- E.M.Forster

Chapter 7: Teachers

What we will cover in this chapter:
- Defining what teaching is
- The primary attributes of an instructor
- The importance of repetition
- Getting the work done
- Keeping to the schedule
- Real world training

So far then we have looked at definitions, structures, personal interaction, presentation, student interaction, and teacher techniques. We know how to teach both students and ourselves now; we understand how to reach them and inspire them, and how to gain as much as them from this process. But what about the actual definitions of what we are doing, and why we are doing it?

This chapter delves a little deeper into the processes and requirements behind the work we are doing and the results we are achieving with our practices. I'm not a formally trained psychologist, but I do understand many of the basics of learning. I am someone who likes things to be explained logically AND by feel, and have reasons for what I am doing at every point, so I can understand what I may also learn to do by instinct.

Training and teaching defined

What can we define as teaching, training, coaching, tutoring, instructing, lecturing, mentoring, or giving information? Aren't these all the same thing?

Well, not quite. In essence you are facilitating a transfer of information, but it's nothing as cold – or reliable – as a copy of data between computers. With humans this is an analogue process, not a digital one, as we are analogue creatures at heart.

Of course some of these methods are virtually the same thing, and have different techniques and amounts of investment from the teacher.

Giving information is the most basic form. It cares nothing for the intake; it is a sharing of data, and there is no feedback, investment or technique. Someone gives you instructions to drive to the next garage; they tell you a set of instructions and that is that. This is not enough in many subjects, or for more than a fleeting interaction.

Teaching is an overall discipline. It can cover a wide variety of subjects, to an astonishing or trivial depth over a long or short period of time, and really can encompass all of the other methods. I have a lot of respect for teachers, and although I have used the term interchangeably in this book with training and instructing, although I am a teacher in the classes, or when I help people elsewhere, I am by no means a trained teacher who can deal with long periods of time and multiple students, developing a long and fruitful relationship which is rewarding for both parties. My time is much shorter, but that doesn't mean I shouldn't try my best to do these things in the time I have.

Coaching, tutoring, and instructing are very similar. These are usually in one particular discipline at a time – a sport, a subject, a solution. This can be one on one or with many students, but it focuses on one discipline usually with a generally set goal in mind of improvement and application.

Training is similar to these, but usually denotes a shorter span for a specific goal. Training in IT for example is a fixed time span to impart details required for doing a job correctly. It can be a general or very specific focus and subject, but it is definitely for a specific outcome. You would train for the Olympics, for example, but you would be coached in the sport you go to the Olympics for. IT courses are generally about training.

Then we have lecturing… I'm not overly sure what to make of this one. It is seen often as quite advanced and usually metaphysical, and the student is expected to already be knowledgeable on the subject and be able to apply the complex, sometimes abstract concepts imparted. I don't find traditional lecturing effective, however good the knowledge of the lecturer – mentoring would be far better - but then the students are supposed to be advanced enough to make their own notes and discern their own order in the chaos.

Finally, there is mentoring – what I see as the best type of teaching. Mentoring can actually be performed in any of the methods. It is interpersonal from a source of deep knowledge and goes well beyond mere information. The teacher supports and guides the student closely but gives them the freedom to advance themselves. I suppose it is the best mixture of all the above techniques, although the type will depend very much on what you are teaching.

Be sure to pick the appropriate technique. Mentoring someone to get to the next garage is waste of time, but mentoring a skilled worker to perform intricate and critical tasks is definitely worthwhile.

There is a lot more to it than these simplifications, of course, but I find these help define the basics.

> *"The aim of education should be to teach us rather how to think, than what to think - rather to improve our minds, so as to enable us to think for ourselves, than to load the memory with the thoughts of other men."* – James Beattie

Techniques for learning – what does the instructor have to practice?

So far we have talked about things a teacher needs to practice to effectively teach, but they haven't been spelt out. Let's take some time to do that.

Everything so far has shown that we should try to maintain excellent patience, reflexes, and quick wittedness; honesty, open mindedness and a willingness to learn. There should be a lack of ego, a drive to inspire, charisma, and humility.

Flexibility, the ability to verbalise a concise summary, inspiration, encouragement and guiding are excellent skills to cultivate. We must be able to move away from the student to allow them to grow themselves, and still be humorous yet remain authoritative without being opinionated.

A teacher should be alert, polite, diplomatic, confident and aware. They should be good at pacing the class. We should be engaging, interesting, passionate, efficient, and prepared; rewarding, knowledgeable or even a guru, professional and last but not least - willing to be wrong!!

So, no pressure.

To be effective you need to TRY to cover the above as best you can, even if it is sparingly and in stages. All of these traits will be tested at times, and some will be naturally easier than others.

> *Looking at these requirements I am amazed anyone manages to be a teacher. You need such a wide swathe of skills and mind-sets that you need to be virtually perfect to conform to all of the above.*
>
> *No one is perfect, and I can assure you least of all me. Whilst I am always honest and open minded, and I value inspiring a class, I have had moments where I have what my grandmother used to refer to as a "brain fart" and just lost my thread completely. Quick wittedness deserts me on occasion, and although I am proud of my patience, on a bad day I may feel a sharp shard of impatience at something or someone. You can deal with it.*
>
> *We are after all only human, but that is a teacher's strength as well as a potential weakness. No one can teach another human as well as a human mentor – at least, not yet.*

The importance of repetition

Very few people retain information fully after learning or hearing it once. The concept may be understood, and some of the data may be remembered, but to firmly embed it in the mind for long term memory most people – myself included – need some repetition. Repetition is the oldest and best learning technique both mentally and physically, but it has different methods of application.

There are precedents as to how much repetition is required. Some people only need a few repeats to get it, and some have prior experience or knowledge which aids memory. Merely repeating something mindlessly can embed a fact, but without context or a trigger it is harder to recall when needed. Repetition over and over within a short timeframe is actually counterproductive as well; this tends to allow you to only remember it in the short term, and serves many students poorly before an exam.

So what is the best way to learn with repetition? From my experience, learning a fact then moving on, then coming back, then moving on further, then coming back later works very well. Every time you come back you recall it a little better and this helps you remember things long term. Many studies have shown that studying repeatedly and sleeping between sessions helps you retain far more data to a far greater level.

For courses this is more applicable to school and longer term learning, as typically we only have 4 days maximum on an IT course; it is very information rich and compact. Ideally the student should also practice and repeat skills this after the course where possible – usually through playing and testing.

This is a limited practice of the *spaced learning* effect where increasing time between repetitions embeds data in memory very deeply. It is sometimes referred to as an obsolete or old technique, being proposed in 1932, but it works very well. The downside is it takes *time,* and today we are very much an "instaculture".

Spaced learning is also how you learn language as a child; you hear adults speaking and you copy them, over and over, learning other words or sleeping in between. We also have interest in this communication, incentive to get things we want, and exposure every day, so no wonder children pick up things more quickly than slightly more jaded adults (who have been indoctrinated into a less intuitive learning pattern for a long time).

Even language as an adult can be quickly learned in situ. You get instant feedback on progress, and you cannot help pay attention and repeat it or have it repeated if you live where the language is commonly used. You are certainly incentivised to learn it! This is less applicable to other subjects however…

> *I believe that it is as important to tell students HOW to study and learn as to make them simply do it; I would have retained a lot more throughout school and college if I had understood spaced learning (and if I'd had the right incentives and understanding).*
>
> *The biggest problem with a lot of the learning I have been subject to in my time is the lack of one of four requirements; incentive, repetition, exposure, and attention. If I simply repeat something I gain limited understanding of it. If I don't care, I may not even do it. I may learn it effectively, but if I don't then use it I forget it. However, if I pay attention while I do it and know I will gain, and I use it regularly, I will get the most from it.*

Getting the work done

As flexible as a curriculum can be made, you MUST ensure you cover the key points in a logical order. You can be personable and present well and relaxed and all the rest of it, but if you don't get through what needs to be done and the class have a gap in what they needed to learn, you have failed as their teacher.

Underneath it all, you are there to run a class. We know by now that it is not as simple as waltzing into a room and throwing information at people before hitting the pub, but you must ensure you cover every single key point.

Depending on the class, I have left out slightly irrelevant – or sometimes quite important! – sections because I have been asked to by a room full of people at the same level from the same partner. In those circumstances it can be done if you are flexible enough. However, this is not best practice, and if something breaks and I am unable to show people something key from the curriculum I am very unhappy and I feel I have not been a good teacher.

Your fault or not – the class need the information. Find a way if you can. I've done everything from breaking out old training laptops wheezing on an outdated Linux running windows VMs and battling with Java to (temporarily) "borrowing" another company's (foolishly unsecured) wireless and sticking a phone on there as a hotspot as well. It may not be pretty, or smooth, but you can almost always get the job done somehow, and you owe it to your students to try.

Keeping to the schedule

Again, this is a balancing act with flexibility – you cannot fall too far behind! The class needs to keep a lively pace to maintain interest but also actually finish within the allotted time span. People may have travelled long distances and have a cut-off point, especially on the last day. People will get bored if you cannot keep the pace up or distract them. If you fall too far behind, you run into the previous section and will have to make a judgement call on what to cut.

Everything in your life may suddenly try and work against you when you run a class. Students, technology, lunch, timing, personal life, health, travel; if it can go wrong it may well do so. I recently flew to Dubai to run a course, and due to some rather unfortunate delays got to my hotel at 4am local time instead of 11pm as planned. I got 2.5 hours sleep, and was at the customers the next morning to train. It was a bit rubbish. It also happens; you have to learn to roll with the punches.

The flip side is true as well. If you (for some reason) end up unexpectedly with 2 people in the class, you may find you progress so fast you have to pad out the course at least a little, to allow them to properly retain the data! Sometimes an overly large class is the smoothest running and fastest course you could want. Sometimes the sudden 3 person class appears beset with delays and problems. Each course is different, and you never know how it will run, so you have to gauge things as you begin and try and finish in the general scope if you can.

This can be particularly difficult sometimes if you encounter excessive technical problems or have an unusually large class, especially if you are training dirty.

Training dirty?

Training dirty is the right way to train. If nothing is going wrong, no one is learning anything! "Clinical" training is not effective. Nothing in the real world happens like it does in the labs. Labs are clean and purpose built. In the real world, a system may have multiple teams of people who hardly talk to each other involved, and something eventually is bound to go wrong.

It is also human nature to play. You would be amazed how many problems over the years have been tracked to people playing with a perfectly good solution without understanding it (they do even sometimes admit to it).

So, in teaching I encourage the students to play, be a little creative. I like people in the class to do their own thing. I very often give them a choice, getting them involved, secure in the knowledge that someone will rush ahead and break something. This is perfect. The class usually chuckles when I yelp, "Excellent! That is EXACTLY what I wanted to happen." And I mean it. If it goes wrong, it teaches you what not to do next time, and I can pull the problem up on the projector and the entire class can get involved in the resolution. The only thing that can beat that for a learning experience is actually resolving it in the real world, bobbing around in the deep end.

If no one breaks anything, through some form of miracle, I will quietly go and break things myself. Of course, remember that the universe equalises everyone eventually – sometimes it ends up being as much of a learning experience for me as it is for them.

Summary

So, we have looked a little bit deeper into the processes and psychology behind the techniques we have covered in previous chapters; what defines teaching and what is required to be an effective teacher. Repetition is critical, but it needs to be done the right way where possible while covering all the key points in the allotted time (elbow room here is your friend!). Lastly – no matter how effectively you train, it is pointless if the information is not applicable in the real world, so make your teaching as real as you can and students won't be caught out later on (and may find it easier to practice).

INVOLVE ME

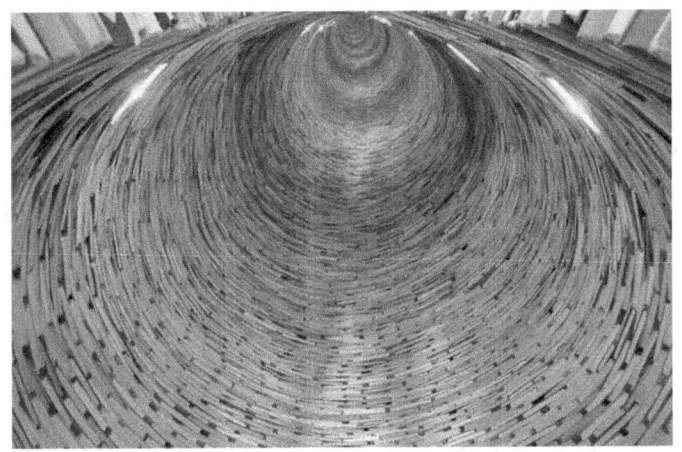

"In learning you will teach, and in teaching you will learn."

- Phil Collins

Chapter 8: Supplements

What we will cover in this chapter:

- Remote training
- Hand-outs and documentation
- Feedback
- Handling Criticism
- Teaching to learn
- Last thoughts

All of the techniques and observations mentioned so far will differ with the delivery method. It is important to understand the differences when teaching face to face versus remotely, and this chapter will look at that, as well as the effectiveness of course documentation.

We also need to understand and deal with feedback from attendees and potential criticism after the course is finished. Although I have called these things supplemental, they are still very important considerations for any course.

Remote or Face to Face?

I am not a fan of remote training. It works to a degree, but many of the techniques in this book are highly impractical if the students are remote.

The trouble with remote training is the investment and interest, or potential lack thereof. As soon as something is in a remote session it is easy to ignore. I am as guilty as the rest of putting up a training session that is an hour of droning PowerPoint and walking off to make coffee, or doing something else with my mind half on it. This is not effective learning.

When students are remote, you have little feedback. You cannot engage or easily establish personal connections. You cannot effectively monitor them, involve them, make them part of the class around the table. Getting investment in the information transfer is more difficult.

You cannot share a screen from one easily with the class and involve them all in troubleshooting. Troubleshooting itself is more work and can take longer. You can't always even tell that they are there!

Face to face training is key for the optimum transferral and retention of information. You CAN train remotely – I have done so – but it is simply not as effective.

It is a little different if one person in 7 is remote, and they are all colleagues – they will have support from the rest of the class and be more involved. I sometimes refuse point blank to teach a whole course remotely however, unless there really is no alternative. It will be so ineffective it will be a waste of time for all involved; far better to schedule time and budget for travelling to train face to face.

> *Face to face teaching represents an actual commitment from someone. If they are prepared to come on the course and take time out, the likelihood is that they genuinely want to learn, and you will cut potential technical problems by half – connection, audio, or visual worries are negated or centrally manageable.*

Hand-outs and why I don't use them

Course documentation is something that can be hard to get right, partially because of effectiveness and partially because of expectation. Traditionally at schools printed hand-outs allow a teacher to quickly and effectively distribute material. The problem is that students often glance at it but don't take it in, or simply read it without realising practical application. It can be helpful, but I think there are better ways to impart information, especially in adult classes and IT.

INVOLVE ME

I believe a much more effective approach is to strongly encourage students to take their own notes, which aids the retention process, and to give them electronic user guides for references and actual tools to perform the tasks if possible. I see no reason to kill trees to give people a door stop which describes when they clicked next – I have had collections of these in the past and they have proved little use in actually using the knowledge I have learned.

Repetition, problem solving, real world application and their own notes (where possible coupled with tools for the real world and reference material) give students a much better chance of retaining and using the information.

Interestingly, this is actually the area I get the least positive response on in the feedback. I used to collect paper this way too, until I realised it is a conditioned response; a trophy of sorts, something that says you have been on the course (as if certificates and knowledge weren't enough!). I eventually realised that as reference it was often pretty poor, and it as burdensome and pointless.

> *I am always interested in why people feel that they should have a binder full of paper, and I often ask why. The response is typically for reference and for sharing with colleagues. I reply that the reference is better laid out and detailed in the user guides, which are electronic and just as accessible for colleagues, and then ask – wouldn't you rather have real world tools that allow you to do the job as I did it? Best practices, spreadsheets, calculators, the presentations I used in the training, the pdf user guides for all the software – isn't that far more effective than paper saying where you clicked next?*
>
> *I think so, and I wish that the courses I had attended had been as pragmatic. When you put it this way, you find most students agree, but you will rarely sway strong traditionalists.*

The importance of Feedback

Feedback is critical to anything you do in life. You need to know what is going on when you do something. In regards to teaching, feedback allows you to spot weaknesses or flaws and make the teaching even better.

One of the best quotes I have ever heard was from Paul McKenna. He said, **"There is no failure – only feedback."** This is brilliant – and true. Feedback teaches you not to make mistakes again, but the most successful people make the most mistakes. The difference is they learn from them and don't repeat them. The only failure comes when you fail to learn from the feedback, and evolve as a person.

It can be hard to get genuine feedback. Some people give good feedback as a reward for training – this is not a favour to the trainer, whatever people think. In the same way that honesty in taking training and an exam is only cheating yourself, having feedback that is nice or irrelevant damages the course in the long term, and may lead the teacher to believe they are more effective than they are. If you give unwarranted good (or bad) feedback, you are doing your teacher a huge disservice.

I don't want feedback that people like me – I want it if I met what they consider a good job, or they loved the lunch, or they felt we didn't cover something, or if there were technical problems. I am very, very clear about asking for honesty, as feedback is what allows me to make the course BETTER. It is natural to want to be good to someone you get on with, but however well I get on with students, in the feedback it is a professional request and I expect as honest an answer as possible.

This is typically not a big problem for me as I train a lot in the Netherlands, and if there is one thing I know about my Dutch friends is it that they will definitely not flatter you for no reason. Blunt understates it. And it's refreshing, welcome, and helpful. If they do not like something, I can CHANGE it if required.

The worst, WORST thing I have had (my only real negative feedback) was neutral-positive from a student, and then he called a regional director to complain that I had eaten food in the training (before lunch – food is delivered to the room), and I had shown content "not subject related".

Don't get me wrong. His criticism is valid. The manner in which he delivered it however was cowardly and unhelpful. The feedback form is there for a reason – use it and be honest, and it benefits everyone.

> *Listen to the feedback, and make mistakes. You're allowed to. You HAVE to. Otherwise you won't learn enough to teach anyone else.*
>
> *"It's much easier, after all, to learn mathematics from someone who's made a few mistakes. It's impossible to learn it from someone who always gets it right." – John Lennox*

How do you handle criticism?

Criticism is a necessary and healthy part of feedback. As long as it is constructive and relevant it should be carefully considered.

A large retail outlet recently condescendingly told me that my comments "had been noted" when I complained (quite politely) about a device I bought. They told me feedback is always important, and then proceeded to ignore me.

The sentiment is noble, but the way in which they approached me was uncaring and defensive. At the merest hint of negative feedback, they fell back on outdated policies as if under attack and quoted near-perfect complaint records (which I doubt are correct). As a result, they have exacerbated the problem to the point I will actively encourage no one to ever buy from them again and they have alienated a customer.

Take it in your stride. If criticism is constructive, you MUST listen to it and judge it for yourself as objectively as possible. No one opinion is correct all the time; it is beneficial to listen to as many as you can to make your own informed judgement.

Don't take negative criticism the wrong way, either. In the example above of the underhand feedback in the previous section, I was then requested to change things on the course on the strength of one student. It is interesting to note that after hundreds of successful and happy students passed through, they were the first one to precipitate a demand for change.

Note, I did not suddenly change the course for this. Negative things catch the memory and are higher profile than positive, for longer periods of time. Again, it's human nature. Listen to your criticism, and if warranted by logic or numbers make changes – but don't do it as a knee jerk reaction to one student.

Is teaching REALLY the best way to learn?

Yes. Purely and simply, to understand a subject to the level required to effectively teach someone else deepens and broadens your understanding in some way every single time you train people. It may be a minor detail, or it may be something new. You may be required to learn revision to previous information, or new solutions.

Dr Richard Mobbs of Leicester University estimates that the percentage of retention of information is:

- A Lecture (5%);
- Reading (10%);
- Audio Visual (20%);
- Demonstration (30%);
- Discussion group (50%);
- Practice by doing (75%);
- Teaching others (90%).

Clearly, then, you learn the most from teaching others, but the next best thing is actual practice. Combine this with Audio/Visual cues and provide reference for reading and you can get the most out of a 1, 2, or 4 day course. If you can encourage the attendees to all help each other – in essence, once they grasp a concept, helping *teach* it – they will retain even more.

Before you can teach others, you must teach yourself to order the information to express it, and that helps you learn even faster next time. I now find I can pick up some related technologies in a matter of hours and prepare a basic course for others, because I understand the intrinsic principles and can fill in the details at relatively short notice. It's not ideal, stuff gets missed, but it CAN be done at a pinch.

In fact it is a hope that when students leave the class, they will train others in their company. Sadly I am all too aware that we have little free time, and it usually ends up as the colleague reading the notes and having a play, but sometimes you get a training session – and while it may not be as comprehensive as that from the horse's mouth, it can still teach them all a lot.

> *Since helping people with indoor climbing, writing, data protection and teaching itself, the gym – in fact, anything I at least partially understand - I have found my own comprehension exponentially increases. It is a fantastic feeling to have the self-imposed limits removed and to see how much you can learn. It is also humbling and a little sad – you realise you will never learn all there is about even one subject.*

Summary

Learn to use as many of the traits outlined in this book as you can. Learn to see students as equals and individuals. Train effectively for the real world. Combine as many of the skills of a teacher as you can, and never stop learning yourself. Follow what you can in this guide when and where you can, and your students will benefit – and so will you.

You will not be able to apply all the techniques in here all of the time. You will have to choose when and what will apply, and how to best deliver it within any confines you may have; every teacher faces different challenges. But if you stick to as many of the core values as you can, you will feel effective and have a sense of achievement after the course, and will have taught the class – and yourself – as best you could.

You also cannot win them all. Not every student will retain information or learn; sometimes they paid no attention due to other work, for example. At least you will know you did everything you could to open than door for them.

As I said at the start, this is not a "train the trainer" or an IT training manual per se, although elements can apply to either. It is simply a set of observations and techniques that I believe make a difference. Hopefully they will for you too; they may not in some circumstances. Not every teacher is the same, nor is every class, but I honestly believe that if you use your sense, use the applicable techniques in this book, and INVOLVE the students… they will UNDERSTAND.

Last thoughts

Learning is core to everything we do, every day. You drive to work, you are learning. You work out, you are learning. You read, you are learning. You talk, you are learning. You go to a class, you are learning, you read a book, you LEARN. You teach… you are LEARNING.

The trick then is how to learn effectively and how to inspire others to do the same. And it is a trick, a technique; the rest is up to the student.

So, I leave you with this final thought:

> *"Learning is but one leg of two for moving forward. The other is applying what you have learned, which is harder than learning; but without both in constant motion, you get nowhere." – Me*

About the Author

Christopher Bramley is an IT Consultant of 17 years' experience. During his time he has worked in call out, 1st to 3rd line support, Pre Sales, Professional Services implementations, partner enablement in the Data Protection channel, expertise in multiple skills, and training/mentoring.  He is also a lazy musician and artist, and spends most of his time reading, researching, training gym, martial arts, rock climbing and writing fantasy books about some rather large dragons. He loves to learn and teach others whatever subjects he knows enough about, and is full of generally useless facts. Don't get him started on nutrition.

You can follow him on Twitter at https://twitter.com/christopbramley (@christophbramley) or visit www.christopherbramley.co.uk for updates on this and his other novels.

www.ingramcontent.com/pod-product-compliance
Lightning Source LLC
Chambersburg PA
CBHW072102290426
44110CB00014B/1793